To Warm Your Heart

Dear Ed —

May the words
in this little book
bring you smiles and
tears — for such is
life —

Katy

To Warm Your Heart

Contemplations
from Ketayun Guard

Many a heart pines only
to fly out of bondage into freedom.

To Warm Your Heart

Copyright © 2010
Ketayun Guard

Written by Ketayun Guard
Edited by Amy A. Dyson
Illustrations by Amy A. Dyson
Cover Design by Nancy J. Bamberger
Author Photograph by Nancy J. Bamberger

First edition 2010
Library of Congress Control Number: 2010936832
ISBN 978-0-615-41477-5

Printed in the United States of America by
CVF Publications
4376 Argos Drive
San Diego, California 92116
www.cambodianvillagefund.org

10 9 8 7 6 5 4 3 2 1

Dedication

This book is dedicated to children.

All proceeds from the sale of this book benefit children's education around the world. By purchasing this book you have helped a child realize the dream of becoming a respected citizen of the world.

Funds will be distributed to these organizations:

Kaivalya Mandiram Trust, partnering with Each One Teach One, helps children in India - www.eachoneteachoneindia.org

The Cambodian Village Fund helps children in Cambodia - www.cambodianvillagefund.org

Through education, may the children's plight turn into play and their hopes into a bright future.

Preface

The book you're about to open
Has nothing that is new.
The words you will read
Have been written or spoken
Some time, some place
We know not where or when,
Therefore, they are not, can not
Be called
"Original."

Enjoy therefore the words before you
Or throw the book away.
If intended for you
It will be read.
No one but you will know,
Not a single soul will care!

Acknowledgements

When you set your heart to help others, the universe works with you to accomplish your goal. Many people came together to create this book.

The words and stories came to Katy as if by magic. Inspired by these stories, Amy Dyson set about organizing the material and her drawings followed. With the support of Bill and Nancy Bamberger, the book became a reality.

Nancy Bamberger, Pamela Goosby, Cynthia Hernandez, and George Weinberg-Harter further refined the work with their insightful and diligent proof reading.

Bill Bamberger and Brian Dyson provided invaluable technical assistance and loving support to help make this project happen.

Many thanks to the Cambodian Village Fund for publishing this book.

Contents

Katy Tea

by Ketayun "G," or Katy for short

Come drink with me – open this book,
Enjoy this brew
Divine.

They call it "Katy Tea,"
Ask not what in it goes.
She hides not the recipe, however,
It's the secret word which stirs
God's energy
Into her brew
Transforming it
To nectar divine
We call "Katy Tea."

Come then, drink with me
This Katy Tea.
More than the hands that hold the cup
It warms the heart!
So breathe the magic in.
Come drink with me
This magic brew,
This Katy Tea.

What is "New?"

"New, new it is," they say,
"Fresh as morning dew!"

New, fresh as dew, you say?
Think well. Where was the dew
Before on leaf it showed its face?

Shape and form may vary,
Appearance may change,
That's not disappearance.
Nothing disappears.

There's nothing new under the sun.
Things may be hidden from view
But they're always there.

Pearls

Did the fisherman know
The pearl was hid
In oyster's crusty shell?

Unseen, unknown, unheard
Great souls remain
Like pearls – untouched.

They seek no name, no fame,
They're revered!
Why leave then footprints on the sands of time?
They soon will disappear.

Charity

You have a pound, and give to the beggar a penny.
You call that charity?
Note the homeless man on the street
Pulling and stretching the blanket off his feet
In order to cover another
More hungry than he.
That is true charity.

The Coin when given,
Brings bread to the beggar.
Held tight in the fist
It hurts palm and finger.

Soar Like an Eagle, Not Like a Kite

Fettered to naught,
Beholden to none,
Soar.
Soar like an eagle
Not like a kite
That dances to the whim
Of him
Who holds the string.

Life, love, liberty,
Who seeks them not?
And yet,
Eyes half-closed
We dream and yearn
To catch
Their slippery limbs.

Hear thee not then
The Whispering Voice?
That soft sweet sound
Waiting to be heard,
"I'm here, right here,
Always here, always now,
Forever and always with thee."

What's that you speak – life, love, liberty?
I'm one, not three.
Can love be
Without life?
And "Liberty" – what's that?
Just a word you've heard.
Who told you you're bound?
You were, and are, Free!

Eyes half open you dream.
You long for that which is not.
Open wide your eyes and see the light
Or shut them tight
And leap,
Leap out of that prison
Mind-made.

Hast heard thou not
The song from the bard –
"Stone walls do not a prison make
Nor iron bars a cage?"

Then shut tight your eyes
And leap -
Wings spread wide -
Soar free.
Soar like an eagle
Not like a kite.

Man's Envy of Wings

Man's envy of bird never has ceased.
For ages the mind has conceived
"If only like a bird I could fly!"

We dream of flights
To faraway places,
To distant shores,
To mountains majestic.

Many a heart, however,
Pines only to fly
Out of bondage
Into freedom.

O'er and o'er again we fancy
Wings will fulfill our dreams.
"If only like a bird I could fly!"

On ladder of evolution
The bird appeared
Eons ahead of man.
From lowly worm
Through insect to bird
Was, indeed, a steep ascent.
Then came the turn of animals to follow -
Last of all came man.

Man, acme of creation is he
But why was he shorn of his wings?
Is it possible an error in God's plan occurred?
Or was this shearing intended?

Man struggles and sweats even before
He takes his very first step.

What crime then did man commit
To deserve such punishment
That his wings be taken away from him
Never, ever, to be returned?

Perhaps it was planned
We remain malcontent
Forever longing, desiring
What we have not.

Perhaps it was thought
This way, we forget not
Our Maker.

One way or another
We will forever
Cherish our dream eternal -
"I wish, I wish I had wings.
I wish, like a bird, I could fly!"

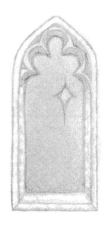

Space Holds All

Thoughts and words
Like arrows released
May fly fast and far,
Think not they've gone away.
The vast expanse we call "Space"
Holds all: The shout in anger made as well as
The mother's lullaby.

Tales For Children

Tales for children have often been writ
To open the ears of the grown-ups.
We think we're smart, we know
And act as we do, creating nothing but
Lots and lots of trouble.

If we swallow our pride and learn
The lessons that these tales do give
The earth will be a much nicer place
On which all of us could live.

The Hare and the Tortoise

The hare and the tortoise
Did one day declare
A race across the meadow.

Sure to win was the hare
Being aware
Of the weight on the tortoise's back.
He nibbled at grasses,
Chased sparrows and finches,
E'en decided to take a few naps.

Reaching the finish line
Amazed was he to find
That the large, heavy tortoise
Was already there!

No matter how heavy your burden may be
Focused, tho' slow, you're going to win.

Two Baby Frogs

Two baby frogs, both brothers, they,
Fell – plunk – into the milk-maid's full pail.

Try as they might, they just could not
Jump and come out.

One baby frog, despairing, stopped trying.
He fell to the bottom of the pail, stone dead.

The other frog,
He kept swimming and flapping around.
He just would not give up.
He kept trying and trying until
The fat separated and from the milk emerged
A large chunk of butter.
On it jumped the frog,
He quickly leaped out,
Jumping away to safety.

What lesson does this story teach you, my children?
Keep trying and trying. Never, ever, give up!

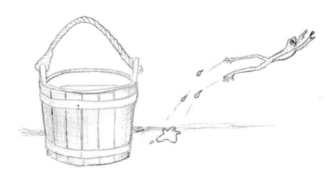

The Lion and the Mouse

The King of the Forest, his belly full,
Lay snoring away in the forest.
A mouse nearby became curious,
He wanted to locate
The source of the rumble
And jumped upon the lion's back.
About to start exploring he was
When suddenly he found
His tiny head pressed
Into the ground
Beneath a Giant Paw.

"Please, please, let me go!" the mouse squealed.
"Please, I promise, I won't do this again!" he cried.
A gulp of pity arose
In the lion's huge throat.
He lifted his paw and let the mouse
To safety, scurry away.

It was a month later
The same giant paw got trapped
Inside a hunter's well-hid net.
Hearing the pitiful roar
The mouse came running
To set his savior free.

For many a day
He kept nibbling away
At last getting the lion free.

Little though he was, he now became
The Giant Lion's Very Best Friend!

The Dog at the Pier

A fisherman and his dog were always together
Never on land did they part.
Side by side they walked each morning
Ambling along on their way to the pier.

The dog would wait there until
Sundown brought master to shore.

A fierce storm one day
Carried ship and master away,
Keeping the dog at the pier
Patiently waiting.

Hour after hour,
Year after year,
The dog stood there and waited,
But the fisherman -
He never returned.

Still standing at the pier
Some years later
The dog laid down and died.

In memory of him
The people erected at the pier
A statue - a beautiful replica, named
"The Waiting Dog."

The Juggler

It matters not
What you offer to God
So long as it's given with love.

There once lived a juggler
A poor man, he,
In a village, a little village
In France.

A devotee of
The Divine Virgin was he,
Adoring her
Passionately.

Not even a sou to offer her
Night after night
He entered the church
And juggled before
His Beloved.

The priest one day found out.
He came and stealthily
Opened the church door.

About to pounce upon juggler was he
For his sacrilegious, defying act
When, taken aback, he saw

The Virgin descend
To lay her ivory hand
Upon the juggler's head
As if to say
Dear one, thank you for your gift,
Come again!

Abashed, amazed,
The priest left the church
Crying his heart out aloud

How wrong, how wrong, can a man of frock be
Believing in his superiority
O'er a penniless juggler?
Far wealthier was he
In the Virgin's love.

The Fire Thrower

Ram was young and immature.

"I will now leave you, Master," he said,
"I've found a teacher
Mightier than you.
He can throw from his mouth,
A stream of fire!"

"Show him to me, Ram,
I must meet this man,
See him perform
Such a miracle!"

Ram took Master to his new-found teacher.
They witnessed a miracle -
Fire spitting out
From a human mouth!

Returning home the Master declared,
"Impressed I am, Ram, to see such great power.
Left to me, however,
I'd waste not twenty years
In study of such art.
After all, it takes me but a second
Getting fire from a match!"

"A man without scruple
May pass off as miracle,
Power acquired by Sidhhi!
Don't let that fool you, Ram.
Refer only to your jewel,
Your very own jewel,
The one we spell
Discrimination."

Ram and the Genie

Ram, a student, from his master received
A powerful gift – a genie.
"He's yours, this genie,
Every wish of yours he'll fulfill.
Remember, tho', all times keep him busy.
If not, he'll die; but before dying
He'll open his mouth and consume you."

The genie stayed busy day and night.
All wishes, smallest to biggest,
Came ceaselessly true.
Palaces of marble, roads paved with gold,
Jewels never seen by man
Started piling high
Before Ram's eye.
He sought all that he loved, loved all that he saw.

Many days later Ram grew weary
Awake he could stay no more.
"What shall I do now?" he appealed to master,
"I have to sleep now or else I'll die!
Help me, Master, please!"

"Very well then,
This tall pole install
In the center of your courtyard.
When Genie asks next for your command
Tell him 'Go up on this pole' and he will.
Once up he'll ask 'What next, master?'
You'll command 'Come down.'
Once down, you tell him 'Go up.'
Up and down let him travel until
He can take it no more
And quietly, in the dead of night,
He'll run away."

"Next time, Ram, be sure what you wish.
If not, you'll be swallowed
In the sea of your very own desires
Never fulfilled!"

Ram and the Tree

Ram and his Guru were walking one day
When suddenly Guru caught hold of a tree.
"Ram, Ram, come quick, pull me!" Guru cried.
"Pull me away from this tree - it grabs me,
It won't let me go!"

Ram pulled and pulled and pulled
But could not set his master free.
Then Guru, laughing, jumped off the tree saying
"Learn well the lesson of the tree.
Man wrongly thinks that troubles, like this tree,
Are grabbing him, holding him down
When in fact it's man grasping the tree
Not the other way around!
No tree on earth has power to hold -
It's the mind of man holding on to his problems
Moaning and groaning always for release."

The Steed You Call "Now"

Ram to his master appealed,
"Help me, master, what shall I do?
How shall I conquer my greatest enemy, Time?"

"More slippery than eel
She slithers away
Today turns into yesterday,
Yestermonth, yesteryear,
How can I conquer this enemy of mine – Time?"

The master replied,
"As the good warrior that you are
Leap high and land on the steed's back,
The steed you call "Now."
Hold her fast between your knees,
She cannot move,
And you, my fearless Ram,
Have conquered Time."

Monkey in the Flood

The forest floor was wet.
She knew, the Monkey Mother knew
Her worst fear was coming true –
The Great Flood!

Screeching, screaming, she gathered her brood.
Four jumped on her back, four clung to her belly.
Drenched to the bone she began her flight
Up the tree, to safety.

The price for this climb, however, was steep –
From branch to higher branch forced was she to leap.

The tree was mighty, however,
The higher she went she found
The branches kept thinning around.

They could not bear the family's weight.
The littlest baby had to be cast, alas,
Into the water below.

She climbed a little further.
Seeing the raging water below, cold turned her blood.
Soon she must give another babe to the flood,

And one more, and one more
Until at last at the top she arrived,
All babies gone, she alone survived.

She had sacrificed them all for her own safety.
She wept in her loneliness, refused to eat,
Pining for her babies she laid down to die
All alone in forest, now dry.

The Healing Mantra

As just reward for good work done
A Sadhaka received from his Master
A most secret healing mantra.
"Such power has it," he was told,
"It can make even a blind man see."

"Remember, however,
It's for you and you alone.
Dare not to share it.
The moment you do
You'll turn into
A pile of ashes!"

No sooner had the Sadhaka left
The village bell was heard
Loudly ringing, summoning all.

The Master came running.
"What are you doing, you fool, don't you know
You'll die if you tell?"

"That I know, Master,
But I, as one, am better dead
If all the lame and all the blind in the village
Will begin to walk
Or start to see
The light of day."

Recognizing the greatness of the Sadhaka
The Master prostrated before him, saying,
"I see now who you are, I remove the curse.
In fact, from now on you will my teacher be
And I your humble Sadhaka."

The Faithful Dog

A king, with queen, a dog and brothers three
Left kingdom and life on earth to be
Close to God, in heaven.

Instructed they were to keep going forward,
No looking back was allowed.

Hard as the journey was
The brothers collapsed and were forced
Home to return.

The King and queen went on, but soon
In extreme heat and thirst
The queen sought to stop and rest.

"No, queen, we must go on -
Not one step back can we dare.
Reach forth your hand, I'll pull thee."

The queen, almost dead, could not
Lift a finger; she fell.

The king went on and reached
Heaven's gate.

The keeper exclaimed
"You are most welcome, King,
But that dog with you
May not pass through.
No animals in here are allowed."

The king replied
"I started with five –
Queen, brothers and dog.
Only this dog, most faithful, with me stayed.
If you deny him entry to heaven
I too will to earth return."

No sooner those noble words left the king's lips
Than the dog, like magic, disappeared
And in his stead stood
The Lord of Heaven, a welcoming smile on his face.

Once Upon A Time

"Once upon a time,"
Those magical words
Ne'er fail to soothe the child
Sending her to Slumberland,

No sooner said
Those words have prepared
The young one to enter into
No Man's Land.

Lids start to droop
Breath becomes soft
Gnomes and fairies
They start to appear

On swift twinkly toes
They dance in the air
Filling the child's dream world
With fun and fanfare.

May seem like a lifetime
Brief moments they are, tho'
They bring mirth and excitement
To the head on the pillow.

"Once upon a Time"
O'er and o'er repeated,
Fresh as the morning dew,
Those words have remained.

The child, now mother,
Says the same four words
"Once Upon a Time"
To the sleepy little head
On the pillow.

Mother

Day after day I'd see her
In Silence, meditating.

"Your kids are grown,
All chores are done.
Why don't you now,
Dear Mom, go around? Travel?"

"My child, you don't know –
I've been there.
I've seen every land,
Been on every sea,
All worlds I have explored -
None can fathom.
Ask me not
To leave my home
Wonders of the earth to seek -
Again, I say, I've been there."

Of course, those days I was younger.
I did not understand -
Couldn't get -
What she meant.

Now I am much older. I see
Her wisdom.

It's in the Quiet,
The Silence,
That a tiny drip of nectar
Seeps
Producing
Something.
A taste? A smell? A touch? Can't tell!
Seems to have no name.
It's beyond
Description –
That Drip of Something –
Incredibly...Wonderful!

Today, therefore, I understand
What my mother used to say.
She'd seen it all,
Explored it all,
She Truly Was – All! My Mother!

Miracles

Don't go searching for them, those miracles,
They always knock at your door.
The baby's smile
Lights your face more than hers.
Is that not a miracle?

The chick emerging from her egg –
Sure, that is a miracle.
But did you hear her pecking in the shell?
She did not stop until
She'd cracked her prison cell.

The foal not a day old
Jumps onto his feet
The minute he is born.
Somehow he knows
His legs unreleased
Will surely cause him
To fall to the ground and die.

Life itself is a miracle.
Every cell in every creature
From birth to death depends
For its very existence
Upon a gift.

This gift so generously bestowed
We've named God's Energy.

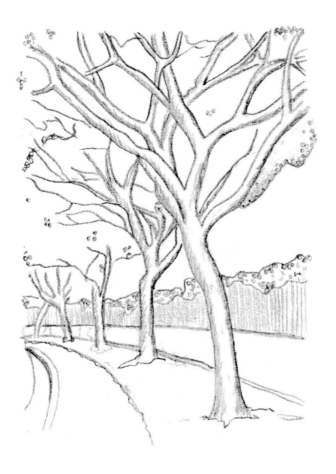

The Green Bough

At every turn of life we find
Nature tries her lesson to give,
But man
If not blind
Is stubborn
And ever refuses to learn.

Take the young green bough -
She is supple,
She bends with the wind.
Once old
With mind of her own
She snaps
In the mildest breeze.

The Seed

Now learn from the seed
How she waits
For the tree to grow,
`Til her patience is rewarded.
Like man if she'd at the start known
Her Potential
Her head would have swollen and
Cracked
Killing the tree in its bud
Prematurely.

The Deer

Learn from the deer.
His musk reveals him,
The hunter's arrow brings him down!

Strut not your charms before the world.
Hid modestly, they will reveal
Like onion skin
One by one
Their beauty on their own.

The Spider

Look not for a teacher
In your bespectacled professor,
Examine the spider instead.
O'er and o'er she weaves,
Going up, going down, round and around,
Silken thread coming out of her body.
She stops not until
Her web's fully done –
A marvel of nature's ingenuity!

The Humming Bird

String after string
Straw after straw
Speedily she flits
From bud to nest
Into the air, and back again, beak-filled,
Faster than anything living I know.
I wonder where and how she finds
These "bricks and mortar" for her babies'
Home.

The River

It's good to watch the river
Dancing down the slope of the hill.
It appears
She meanders
Having a mind of her own.

In fact, however, it's the banks -
They decide the shape she takes,
The girth and depth of her water.

So it is with us humans.
We think we plan our future
When, in fact, it's the hand of fate,
She determines what we do tomorrow.

Ripe Fruit

The fruit when ripe is bound to fall.
Stretch not your arm to pull it down -
That only wastes your time, besides
The unripe pear tastes sour, not sweet!
Sit patiently and wait,
In its own sweet time
Let it descend.

The Ear of Corn

The ear of corn does teach thus –
The seeds on the cob taste not sweet
Till the dry rough husk is shorn.

The Flower Laden Bough

Contrived,
Nothing looks lovely.
True beauty shows
Only when left
Untouched.

A bonsai plant sure is pretty
But can't compete
With the flower-laden bough
Swaying in the wind
Free as a sprite.

Jungle Animals' Hierarchy

Animals in jungles
Adhere, they do, to a very special
Hierarchy.

The tiger makes the kill,
Takes many days to fill
His belly, then walks lazily away.

Only then will approach
Lesser animals, daring
To feast upon the prey.
Finally, when the hyena gobbles down
Long and bloody entrails,
The vulture descends
On the carcass to tear
Whatever remains.

Satiated, the vulture moves slowly away
Allowing the worms finally
To crawl around, do their thing, which is
To bring balance to the earth,
Restoring equanimity.

In that way you see there's order in nature.
This jungle hierarchy
Keeps, in fact, balance and peace.
Each animal awaits his turn
Rushing not, like man,
To be the first
To win the race.

The king once fed
Walks, quite regally, away.
Does he, like man
Gorge himself to death?

You see, there's no greed in Nature -
Each animal comes, takes his share,
Leaves the rest for others.

Even the worm, though low
On nature's ladder may be,
Does his work, unlike us, diligently,
Finishing off the dregs of the kill,
He leaves the jungle floor clean.

This animal story tells us much.
Man may be at the zenith of Life.
Judge by his actions, though, where he truly stands
On God's mighty ladder of creation.

List Not To Them

List not to them, my sweet,
They of little wisdom.
Gathered at the well, like sheep they bleat,
Babes on their backs,
Their men in the fields.

They say I love thee not
`Cause hour after hour I spend in the temple
Praying and honoring my God.
List to them not,
In thine heart do know
I could not love thee, my sweet, so much
Loved I not my God more.

For it's He that opens my eyes each morn
To find dark curls spread across my heart
Their perfume giddying my senses.
It's He who gives me the joy of my breath:
"Here, son, here give I thee one more day.
Love it, live and cherish it,
By e'entide it'll be no more."

Each night I gaze upon the stars, they twinkle,
They wonder why like me thou wakest not
To enjoy them with thy dark almond eyes.

I love thee, dear, more that I love
The stars, more than the moon,
E'en more than the sun.

List not to them, my sweet, do know
I could not love thee dear so much
Loved I not dear God, our God, more!

Arjun Saw Krishna as God

When to Arjun Krishna revealed his true form
Arjun, despondent, fell on his knees, crying,
"Lord, my Lord, please forgive me!
I treated you poorly."

"Thinking you were my friend, I jostled with you
Played with you as my equal!
How wrong I was, I beg your pardon.
Please, please, dear God, forgive me."

Bending down, Krishna raised His beloved Arjun
"Know this Arjuna, I love you most dearly
Because you are my friend.
No use have I of respect or adoration.
Those offering me that, fear me.
Love, love, that is all I ask,
Love and love alone can I give."

"When they follow me they bother me –
I have to wait till they come and reach me,
Or I have to keep turning around to see
They come to no harm."

"When you as friend walk alongside me
It gives me great joy.
Trusting each other we move together
Knowing each other inside out."

"Arjun, my beloved, remain forever
My true, trusting and trusted friend,
Dear Arjun, my beloved friend."

Labor of Love

God does the thinking and planning,
Leaving the joy for us
To wonder and adore.
Why then do we the thinking cap don?
Just to pull His gorgeous Labor of Love
Down?

Luggage on Your Head

Don't place heavy luggage on your head and think
The Train will then go faster.

Let him who plans your fate
Carry it.
Let Him take care of your burden.

The "Gods" of the Hindus

The Gods of the Hindus
Appeal to head or heart.
With so many to choose from
Who can say "There is no God?"

If Kali's too fierce
Turn to Krishna.
His heart like butter
Melts yours!

Or think of Shiva and dance.
In rapture go round and around
Singing "Shiva, Shiva, Shiva
You've stolen my heart."

Lord Narayan, however,
My favorite remains.
Pervading the universe
I find him everywhere.
Eyes open or closed, He is there
Permeating
Every cell.

None, then, can deny
And cry "There's no God."
Pick up your palette
And select
The one of your choice.
He or She – is Yours!

Where Shall We Hide?

In heaven once a meeting was held.
"Where shall we turn?" the Gods did ask.
"Which secret cave, which corner dark
Will protect us
From man's insatiable, ne'er ending
Desires?"

"Tallest mountain, deepest sea,
Jungle filled with wildest beast
Already he has found.
Where then, Oh where, oh where
Can we hide?"

Then did Lord Indra intervene:
"I know a place, brothers, he'll never look.
Go directly there and sit
In the very center of his heart.
For there he never even dares
To peep!"

Let God Do His Work, You Do Yours

This wise man called "Baba"
Had no other name,
He sought no fame
Yet many came to his door
For his wisdom.

I was ten or twelve that time
Visiting Baba for his blessing.
"Baba," I said, "it worries me
I do no good in this world."

Baba waited a moment, then asked
"I see, dear one, but tell me about the bad.
Do you do anything bad?"
"No, I try not to," I answered.

Quick came his answer:
"Good, good, that's fine,
Continue doing what you do."

I remembered his words, didn't argue,
Although unsure of their wisdom.

Now when I hear the words from the mouth
Of a modern sage
I see Baba's wisdom.
The modern sage says
"The sorrows of the world are man-made.
Only man can remove them."

You can't change anything
Other than yourself, your attitude.
Let God do His work, you do yours.

The world would improve
With such counsel followed through:
"Let God do His work
You do yours."

God Alone is the Doer

To no sage say
Thou didst this or that,
It merely shows your vainglorious pride.
The Poem was writ, the Music composed
By God.

To man don't ascribe deeds of valor and virtue.
God alone is the Doer,
Man, they say, the non-doer.

Puppets are we,
We dance to the wish of the Puppeteer.
It's His will, not ours
That moves the earth
Round and around and again, around.

Accept your error
E'en if unsure.
The meek, the humble, sure please Him
And reach His door
I've heard.

It costs you nothing
To swallow your pride and say
"I was wrong."

Let the other man win
And he'll say – with a smile –
"I'm glad I won today
And wish you, my friend,
Better luck next game."

Lakshmi Comes Your Way

The Hindus are right. They say:
When Lakshmi comes your way
To place red dot, a mark of grace,
Run not first to wash your face
You'll miss your chance to become wealthy!
Remain absolutely still,
Receive her blessing.

"I AM"

The only thing you can be sure of is
Your Existence.

You say "I am" and that alone is certain, a kind of
"Truth."
Let me explain this way:

You wake up each morning and say
"I am, here I am."
That "I am" is your Existence.

Of Existence only
Can you be certain,
All else, I say, all else is
Hearsay or Inference.

"What nonsense." You ask,
"Weren't you born? Don't you have
A mother, a father?"
I'll answer, "My friend, that's hearsay.
You were 'told' you were born,
Let's say, on the 5th of November,
On that day, sure, that shape 'appeared.' "

That shape one can see and, therefore, one may say:
"She was born on the 5th of November."
But think – where was this "she" before?

If, in that way, you think and ponder
You find that everything you take for "Fact"
Is only "Fiction."

Once more, I repeat,
The one Fact is
Your existence.

Wasn't Johnny or Danny,
Not Peter, Not Paul that woke this morning.
It was Me. I woke up. That was me.
I know for sure it was me, none else.

That, my friend, is Surety.
Believe in that – "THAT I AM"
For that's the only truth
All else, hearsay or inference.

To Be Born a Human

The human alone
In all creation
Is blessed with power to believe
Making birth in human womb
The finest gift
A creature could receive.

Each time you count your blessings
Breathe deep, give thanks
For this power received,
Placing you at the acme
Of creation.

This power, though, is a dual-edged sword
To be dealt with extreme care.

Thought, word, then deed,
That is the perfect order.
Let thought precede word
Though action may not follow.
If word is merely a silent prayer
Even then let mind review it.

This order of thought-word-deed
We call discrimination,
The crest jewel bequeathed
Exclusively to man.

Fiction Versus Fact

It all began as friendly play
`Tween Fiction and Fact
One dull, wintry day.

"Through one ear, you,
In the other, I,
Together we'll speak
And thoroughly, completely, confuse him,
This vainglorious giant who thinks
He is so smart!"

This game that started as mere play
Has not to this day ended.
We continue to believe
That which is false,
Paying no heed
To the Truth.

The Opposites

Let young lovers play their childish game,
"She loves me, she loves me not,
She loves me, she loves me not."
The petals fall one by one -
The flower gives clue to their future.

Leave that game for children.
In wisdom do learn
The Lesson of the Opposites.

No crystal ball is needed, no guessing game either,
The knowledge is certain:
All things are seen
By their opposites.

Light reveals darkness,
Joy points to sorrow,
Know for sure nothing "is"
Unless another "is not."

Firm in this knowledge
The wise live their lives
In peace and contentment
Aware of the truth
That nothing can ever exist
Without its opposite.

Learn from their wisdom,
The wisdom of the sages.
They leave little to chance
Certain in their choices.

The Mind Plays Games

Simplicity's the answer to all our problems.
There is, there will be
One, just one.

Our convoluted mind,
Not knowing this, keeps seeking, searching,
And just does not find.

Blame not the choices placed before you -
Of course, they will confuse you,
That's why they are there!

Who designed those choices?
Which mischievous imp? Where hides he?
Again you might see

'Twas two, or three or four –
Started playing their game
To make the human quite mad.

All night you stay awake
Looking for the right word,
None other will do.

The brain tosses and turns until
Voila, it appears, right there,
The right word, before you!

Now, you tell yourself, now I will sleep
Only to find
Another tricky thought
Comes to your monkey mind!

Thus on and on, all night, all day
Mind plays games.
Why, you may ask?
Of course, to please itself!

Where Does She Hide, My Soul?

"To thine own Self be true." Well said,
But where, oh where, shall I find?
Where do I seek
My soul?
I close my eyes, and realize
The more I try, the deeper she hides
From me, the unfortunate seeker.

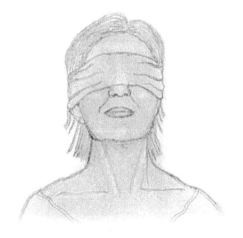

King Janaka And His Vazir

Muddled, befuddled, King Janaka ran
To his vazir, the Wise Vasishta,
"Last night, vazir, in my dream
I found I was a beggar.
Waking up I saw I still was king.
Tell me, wise friend, which am I,
Beggar or King?"

The wise man replied:
"Both and Neither are you, oh, King.

Just and good are you, behaving
Just like a king.
But know you not, you'll one day die
No more to be king?"

"Aha, Vashista, I see :
I am not a king nor beggar,
Dispassionate Witness am I!"

"With that remark, oh King, you display
Your very last illusion: that you are
Superior to your subjects, a GNANI!
As long as such thought exists, oh King,
You are on the level of the mind,
Stranger to Reality."

"I regret, my king, the bearer to be
Of such dismal prophecy."

Just Be

My friend, I tell thee,
Be, just be.
Stop trying and just be.
Let shoulders hang, let eyelids fall,
Give up and surrender.
Just be.

The milk was there
Sweet and warm
E'en ere you slid
Upon the earth.
Before you raise the brow to frown
Remember

All you need is there.
JUST BE.

Meditation

It's no great feat
In forest deep
To meditate. Can you
In busy street,
In crowded store,
Explore
Dark pools of your mind?
I call that Meditation.

Stone Walls

Stone walls for some may not a prison make.
The wise man comes out wiser,
The fool a greater fool.

Life Can Be Fun

Life can be fun, it can be a joy
Only if you let it.
If much you think
You're bound to sink
Dragged into the well
Of your desires.

The Dams We Build

It's the dams we build
with our thoughts,
They halt not,
The waters raging behind them.
Drop by drop, instead,
Ever more and more
The thoughts keep leaking out.

Dive Deep

Dive deep, ponder long,
Every moment of your life watch.
Each in-breath receives what
Out-breath gives,
Peace.
In equal measure that thou givest
Thou receivest.
Nothing is ever lost.

Wait

Droplets sliding off a leaf
Caused Strauss to write
His world famous waltz,
So too, wait in patience and you'll hear
The sound of silence.
After all,
"They also serve who only stand and wait."

Only the Poet Can Hear

The dry seed may fall
On soft grass, and make
Not a sound, not e'en a whisper.
The poet alone can decipher
In his heart, its melody.

The Shoe Pinches

Forge ahead, just do
What you have to do,
For others' views don't care, after all
You're the only one to say
"My shoe pinches here, not there."

The Hem of the Dress

The hem of the dress
Goes up and down
At the whim of the designer.
Follow her trend, you're sure to find
Your coffers get lighter and lighter.

A Convoluted Mind

Judge not the book by its cover.
The bishop's cassock may hide
A convoluted mind.

Judge Not the Bird

Judge not the bird by his feathers.
Wait for spring,
Hear his voice reach his mate,
Then follow their flight
Side by side, towards heaven.

Don't Point a Finger

No matter what you think
Don't be eager
To point a finger
For when you do,
One finger may mark another
While the other three point at you!

The Camel

Like the camel, don't stick your head
In the sand.
Dull-witted, he thinks he is hiding
When, in fact, he's thus becoming
An easy target for his enemy!

Don't Pull the Wool Over Your Eyes

Not knowing who he is
Man pulls the wool over his eyes
Believing himself to be
That which he is not!

The Cap Always Fits You

You've heard it said,
"Wear the cap if it fits you."
No mirror, however,
Is needed for that.

Place cap on head, pull it down, you'll find,
More often than not,
It perfectly fits you!

Perspectives

What's meat for one may be poison for another.
The spider's web glistening golden in the sun
Brings wonder to our mind
But the fly caught within suffers like the Jew
During World War Two,
Caught,
Awaiting extinction.

Pebbles under the Bed

A rich man came to a peasant's home one day
Just to say "Hello."

As they sat down, they heard
Two dogs fiercely fighting.

The peasant reached under his bed
For some rocks at the dogs to throw.

"Fool, you fool," yelled the visitor.
"Know you not these are nuggets of gold?"

"Gold, what is gold? I know not.
The other day I found these rocks
As I walked along
A river bed!"

Reading this tale the learned one
Would declare:
"Throw not pearls before swine."

Reader, however,
Like peasant bend down
To remove, first,
Cobwebs under your kingly bed
And reach
Reach for the lessons you need to learn
From the story.
The lessons they hide
Behind cobwebs you have built,
Unfortunately,
Inside your kingly head.

The Diamond

Its rarity gone
The diamond's not prized at all.
Like sand by the sea
It'll be totally ignored.

Aging – The Divine Way

Is it possible that God,
Like me, is getting on in age?
Is His hearing, like mine,
Declining?

Or, is He wise and, like me,
Merely pretending?

There is so much noise and chatter around us
It should, driving us mad, make us yearn
For peace and quiet. Instead,
Day after day, night after night,
All we do is
Add to that clutter,
Hoping to be heard thus
Better and faster
Than the other!
That's why perhaps
The grey hairs say,
"I never did hear that!"

The sage confirms this wisdom
Repeating
"I speak no lies because
I hear no lies!"

Nature's Way

When beauty departs
Wisdom steps in.
Balance is always restored
'Cause that's Nature's way.

Don't waste precious tears
On what has gone by -
Another will take its place.

Life must go on
'Cause it's Nature's way.

Good Wine

Waste not your youth on prattle,
know for sure
Good wine takes many a year
To mature.

Words

Words, words, words.
They can be your best friends
Or worst enemies.
They may lift you to heaven
Or push you into hell
Uplift you with majesty
Or throw you into despair.

Use them with utmost care
Or, if unsure,
Don't use them at all.

There's a purpose to words
Of course.
This purpose served, remain
In silence.

Sharper than sword
It can pierce – the word.
That wound goes deep,
Robs you of sleep,
Better, then, to remain
In silence.

Lovers holding hands
Share a common message,
They need no words to say
"I love you."

Why, then, waste good breath? You need no words.
Bow low your head
At end of each day
And recall
Blessings received –
Silent messages
From God.

Save Thy Breath

Ere openeth thy mouth
To bring forth a sound
Do know
`Tis no use
To let good air
And precious breath
To waste go.

And worse, that word you'd planned to speak
May have hurt, not healed
Thy friend
E'en, perhaps made him thy foe.

The Four Imperatives

(or call them "suggestions")

Four, no more,
Are the sage's suggestions.
Let them, these four, life's beacons be.
"What will they bring me?" you ask,
"Not much," he says, "just a smile.
A small, sweet smile.
But remain, it will, on your face
Permanently!"

Let's start at Number One. He says
"Avoid the Unnecessary,"
In other words, clutter not your life.
Walk away from the un-needed –
    Thought, word and deed.
Keep the path open and clear.

"Live an Orderly Life" -
That's the second suggestion.
All I can add is, "Just try it!"
Start cleaning out cobwebs,
The webs of the spiders still lurking
In the dark corners of your mind.

"Anticipate not" – that's the third -
"Not pain nor pleasure,"
Follow always this advice.
It draws you away
From the mire
Of fear and desire.

The sage's fourth, and last, suggestion:
"Don't repeat mistakes!"
Aware the sage is
of man's humanity.
"To err is human, of course," he says,
"But, please, please learn!
Learn from those errors -
Don't repeat them.
It's then that you'll sigh
Seeing sorrows piling high
Upon your little head."

Live your life with these four -
They'll keep you for sure
Sane and, above all, secure!

The Seven Gates

Your home is your castle
Your head is your home,
Take care of it night and day.
Post guards, fierce and strong,
At all seven gates – your eyes, ears and nose
Above all, your mouth.

Ensure none enters your castle through any gate
Without your express permission.

Only then will you see
Your own senses changing
Becoming more pure
Thus to ensure
Clarity of mind,
Sanctity of deed and thought.

Thy Dirty Clothes

Afraid, afraid art thou
To shed thy dirty clothes, my friend?

Son of King,
Prince Divine,
Recall
Thy ancestry.

Shed all,
Shed all thou needest not,

Princely robes will then be placed
Upon your shoulders wide.

You'll recognize, and clearly see
Your fears and ugly thoughts
Had no reality.

Walk forth with steady gait,
Remember who you are,
Son of King
The Ruler
Eternally!

The Muse

When the Muse grips you
Look not at the clock and ask
Is it three, or four, or five in the morning?
No, wide-eyed, inspired,
Write, and recall,
"The moving finger writes
And having writ, moves on."

When the Muse approaches
To whisper poems in your ear
Don't go looking for the right paper.
Quickly jot down what she says
Or else, those words are sure
To disappear.

If this book touches one, it has done its job.

All proceeds from the sale of this book benefit children's education around the world.